the new guide to identity wolff olins

The Design Council

The Design Council is recognised by the Government as the UK's national authority on design. The Council's main activities are the commissioning of research projects on design-related topics, particularly stressing design effectiveness to improve competitiveness, communicating key design effectiveness messages to target audiences and developing the Education and Training Foundation, which has a broad remit covering all aspects of design education and design in education.

The Design Council is also copublishing a programme of books with Gower in the allied fields of design management and product development.

The Design Council

the new guide to identity wolff olins

How to create and sustain change through managing identity

Gower

Published by
Gower Publishing Limited
Gower House, Croft Road
Aldershot, Hampshire GU11 3HR
England

Gower
Old Post Road, Brookfield
Vermont 05036, USA

Reprinted 1999, 2002, 2006

British Library Cataloguing in Publication Data

Olins, Wally
The new guide to Identity – Wolff Olins :
Corporate Identity, Retail Identity, Brand Identity, Organisational
Identity, the Corporate Brand, the Corporate Vision and the
Central Idea – How to Create and Sustain Change Through
Managing Identity
I. Title
659.285

ISBN 0-566-07750-7 Hardback
ISBN 0-566-07737-x Paperback

Library of Congress Cataloging-in-Publication Data

Olins. Wolff.
The new guide to Identity – Wolff Olins : corporate identity, retail
identity, brand identity, organisational identity, the corporate
brand, the corporate vision and the central idea : how to create
and sustain change through managing identity.
    p.   cm.
Rev. ed. of : Wolff Olins guide to identity. 1984.
Includes bibliographical references.
ISBN 0-566-07750-7. — ISBN 0-566-07737-x (pbk.)
1. Corporate image. I. Olins. Wolff. Wolff Olins guide to Identity.
HD59.2.0423 1995
659.2'85—dc20   95-20750
                                           CIP

Designed by Wolff Olins
Printed in Great Britain by The University Press, Cambridge.

Contents

Introduction

Identity takes off

In 1983 corporate identity in Europe was just emerging from the obscurity of its graphic design roots and showing signs of mutating into a significant management resource; the United States perhaps was a few years ahead. Although a few big companies in Britain and elsewhere - Bovis, P&O, BOC, Lucas, Renault and so on - had developed large-scale corporate identity programmes, these were still unusual and, in some industries like construction, unique.

It was at this point in the development of European corporate identity that Wolff Olins was asked by the Design Council in London to write a simple, clear guide to the corporate identity resource; to explain what it was and how it could be used.

That seems almost a lifetime ago; how things have changed!

Today it is of course commonplace for corporations and the divisions, subsidiaries and brands which they own and control to operate sophisticated identity programmes. Virtually every large publicly quoted industrial and service company has its own identity. Every high street, for better or worse, every shopping mall and increasingly every airport too, flaunts the identities of the major banks and retailers, often in a mind-numbingly repetitive fashion. Every channel on every TV station has its own identity, some of which are most ingenious and compelling. Every event from a gig to a motor show has a specially created identity. You can't walk along a high street, read a newspaper, look at TV, go on holiday or wander into a shop without stumbling over identities (or 'idents' as they seem increasingly to be called) of one kind or another.

Identity has now moved way beyond the commercial area. We live in a world in which opera companies, orchestras, charities, universities, film companies and football clubs all have identities too. In addition, in an increasingly nationalistic and in some ways fragmented era, the city, the region and the nation are developing full-scale identity programmes, partly to encourage self-confidence and self-esteem and partly to attract inward investment and tourism.

In fact these days it's pretty difficult to think of any activity involving more than two or three people that doesn't have a name style, logotype, some colours and sometimes a more, or often less, comprehensive guide to its use.

Identity in its various manifestations has grabbed the hearts and minds of those of us who live in the last few years of the twentieth century, because all of us are desperate to express our need to belong and overtly to differentiate ourselves and our aspirations from those around us.

Identity and the corporation

Meanwhile the identity of the corporation itself has become an even more important issue than ever before. The MORI research company conducted a survey in 1992 amongst chairmen of some of Europe's biggest corporations. The results were both interesting and significant. Corporate identity emerged as one of the main concerns in the minds of the people who ran these companies. They were certain that the corporate reputation affects recruitment, acquisitions, sales, collaborative agreements and many other parts of corporate life, including, in particular, share price.

Despite all this, many executives admit that they still do not know how to place a value on identity or how to manage it and control it. There isn't any indication that senior people within an organisation understand how or why the perceptions of their company improve or worsen. Some companies still do not know who to turn to for help in managing their identity activities. They are not aware that identity is a major resource for instituting and managing change. It's quite extraordinary that a resource which is generally regarded as so significant, and is now so ubiquitous, is so little understood.

Identity consultancies

The companies which produce all this identity work, mostly design consultancies with a bias towards graphics, but some PR companies, advertising agencies, marketing consultancies and other specialists too, have not made the job of explaining the identity activity any easier. In fact many of them have compounded the confusion. They are all anxious both to differentiate their work from that of their competitors and to claim for it unique characteristics and advantages. So they coin all kinds of variants around the words corporate, identity, strategy, image, brand and design. That's why we hear about organisational identities, corporate voices, retail identities, brand identities, corporate identities, strategic design and, with increasing frequency, corporate branding.

In addition to their desire to differentiate themselves from each other, which is, as I have indicated, a rich source of confusion, there are two other issues which exacerbate the situation. The first is that many of the consultancies purporting to practise identity stem from different backgrounds – some from marketing, others from public relations and most from design. Inevitably they use words and phrases deriving from their own disciplines: these are semantic differences. But second, and more important, there are some conceptual differences between them as well. Those consultancies stemming from the marketing and communications field will regard identity primarily as a marketing resource linked to branding. They will talk in the main about corporate branding. Others based around the graphic design discipline will still talk about house style or even corporate livery.

Identity and the management of change

The major conceptual change, however, is much more fundamental. Increasingly identity is being adopted as a management resource by organisations involved in behavioural change who are finding that such changes can work better and faster when they are supported by visual change. Equally, identity consultants involved in external manifestations of change are discovering that visual change only makes real sense if it represents and symbolises behavioural change.

This development, the importance of which cannot be overemphasised, is indicative of a growing maturity in the identity business and the beginning of a recognition of its multi-disciplinary character. However, there is no doubt that, at least as things stand, it is cause for some conflict and misunderstanding.

Because of this turmoil, which is probably quite healthy, I can think of no other area of management activity in which such widespread use is accompanied by equally widespread confusion.

Updating the Guide

The whole area of identity activity is vast and diffuse. Identities are now widely applied in both private and public sector activities and to geographic and ethnic entities. In addition, as I have indicated, there is a growing gulf between internally or behaviourally directed identities and externally or marketing directed identities. There are, however, an increasing number of highly significant identity programmes which, with great success, encompass both internal and external areas. It is clear that this is the long-term direction. The identity discipline will, over time, embrace organisational behaviour as firmly as it has

embraced and been embraced by marketing. The sooner that
this is recognised the better.

Despite the fact that the identity activity has won its struggle
to be recognised as a significant management resource, the
misunderstandings and confusions about its role, both inside
and outside the organisation, remain as great as, perhaps
greater than, ever which is I suppose the justification for this
latest expanded and completely revised edition of
The Wolff Olins Guide to Identity.

Wally Olins
September 1995

Definitions and guidelines

Much of the terminology used within and around the identity activity is loose and sloppy. The terms corporate identity, corporate reputation, corporate image and corporate personality are used more or less indiscriminately and interchangeably by many people who talk and write about the subject and who should know better, including no doubt myself.

Corporate personality, corporate identity, corporate image, corporate reputation and organisational identity

Many years ago in *The Corporate Personality (Design Council, 1978)* I wrote that *corporate personality* is the soul, the persona, the spirit of the organisation manifested in some comprehensible way.

I wrote then: 'The tangible manifestation of a corporate personality is its corporate identity. It is the corporate personality under cultivation.' *Corporate identity,* then, is the explicit management of all the ways in which the organisation presents itself through experiences and perceptions to all of its audiences.

Corporate image is what all the audiences of the corporation perceive of the identity which has been created and projected.

Corporate reputation is the reputation enjoyed by the organisation amongst its different audiences.

Because the identity resource has now been adopted by organisations of all types, many of them quite remote from the corporation, the term *organisational identity* is increasingly and rightly being used.

Corporate branding

When people talk of *corporate branding,* they usually mean the corporation or part of the corporation treated as a brand and aimed at the customer.

Inevitably then, because it is primarily and sometimes exclusively focused on external audiences, corporate branding either ignores the internal audience of the organisation or, more often, gives it a much lower priority.

A few rules

Identity has now become a significant mainstream management activity. It can be, although it isn't always, a complex, multi-faceted and multi-disciplinary process. Identity can be a marketing resource, a design resource, a communications resource or a behavioural resource either consecutively or collectively. All this makes it pretty difficult to pin down.

Identity activity is associated with a few simple rules which I have tried to outline in this Guide.

These are that identity:

- is about enabling change to happen and emphasising that change has taken place
- deals with both internal and external audiences
- is a design, marketing, communication and human resources tool
- should influence every part of the organisation and every audience of the organisation
- is an economical resource because it mostly co-ordinates what already exists or what has to be done.

the new guide to identity

Section One

What it is

What is identity?

Every organisation carries out thousands of transactions every day: it buys, it sells, it hires and fires, it makes, it paints, it cleans, it promotes through advertising and other publicity – and so on. In all these transactions, the organisation will in some way be presenting itself – or part of itself – to the various groups of people with whom it deals. The totality of the way the organisation presents itself can be called its identity. What different audiences perceive is often called its image.

So all organisations have an identity whether they explicitly manage it or not and whether they are aware of it or not.

Because the range of corporate activities is so vast and the manifestations of identity are so diverse, the identity cannot normally be managed as a whole unless active steps are taken to do so. Thus, identity management can be defined as the explicit management of all the ways in which the organisation presents itself to all of its audiences. The key word here is explicit.

Identity can project four things:

- who you are
- what you do
- how you do it
- where you want to go.

Identity manifests itself primarily in three main areas which you can see:

- products and services – what you make or sell
- environments – where you make or sell it
- communications – how you explain what you do.

And one which you can feel and can sometimes almost see:

- behaviour – how you behave – to your employees and the world outside.

A pre–WW2 BMW 327 coupé and a 1995 BMW 850 coupé. The sleek and aggressive style of BMW cars, which goes back to the 1930s has strongly influenced the company's image.

Products/services

Sometimes the product and how it performs are by far the most significant factors in influencing how the organisation as a whole is perceived. It is, for example, the appearance and performance of a BMW car which largely influence the way we perceive the image of the company that makes it.

Many organisations deliberately design their products/services with their identity in mind. Sony's identity is based around the products it designs and makes. We pay just a little more for Sony's products because they look good and perform well.

Environments

In some organisations, like retail stores, hotels and leisure centres, the environment is crucial in presenting the idea of the organisation to its customers. Holiday Inns' identity derives largely from the environments which it consistently seeks to create. We know, as hotel guests, more or less what a Holiday Inn will be like. We have expectations which form our image.

All organisations have offices, canteens, factories or other places in which staff live and carry out their work, and these exercise a powerful influence on the way both employees and outsiders see the organisation. That, for example, is why banks' headquarters are traditionally intended to project stability, influence and wealth. The headquarters of the Hong Kong Shanghai Banking Corporation designed by Sir Norman Foster, and for a time the

The head office of the
Hong Kong Shanghai
Banking Corporation
designed by Sir Norman
Foster, projecting an
image of size, style
and power.

tallest building in Hong Kong (until 'outsized' by
another bank), is one of the more recent examples
of this tradition. The bank uses its head office building to display its power and style, both to its own
people and to all outsiders who come into contact
with it.

Communications

There are some organisations in which the communications process is the prime means by which the
identity emerges. Coca-Cola, like many fast-moving
consumer brands, has an identity largely created
and consistently fostered through promotion and
advertising on an immense scale over a period of
more than 100 years. That's why people say that
Coke has a powerful brand image.

More unusually, Benetton, a manufacturer and
marketer of uncontroversial clothes, has gained
remarkable notoriety through highly controversial
advertising and promotion. It uses communications
to promote an idea of itself beyond what it makes
and sells. Through its communications, rather than
through its products or environments, it makes
us aware of who and what it is and seeks to be
as a corporate entity.

Every company communicates, both to its own
staff and to a variety of outside audiences. In addition to personal voice and mail, the communication
process embraces all the printed material that the
organisation uses, from invoices through to press
advertising, together with communication in other
media, TV, events, new product launches and so on.
The totality, nature and content of the communication process influence the way in which different

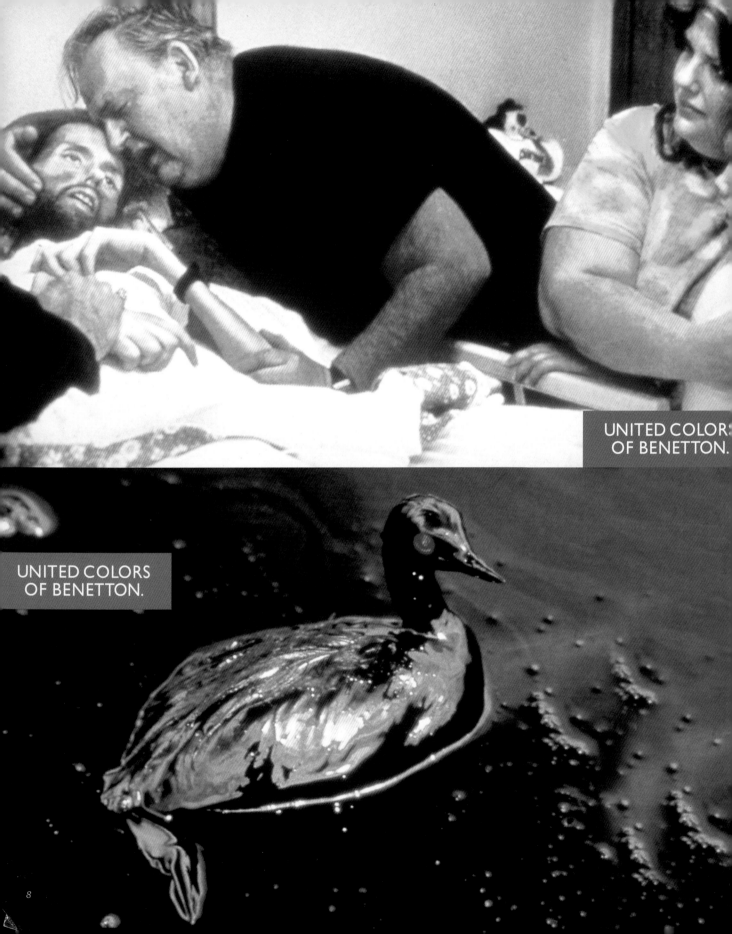

UNITED COLOR:
OF BENETTON.

UNITED COLORS
OF BENETTON.

8

audiences perceive the organisation. So if an organisation uses e mail it implies a sophisticated approach to technology and change.

Behaviour

There are some organisations whose personality and style emerge not so much through what they make (product) or where they live (environment) or through the images they use to promote themselves (communication) as through the way in which they behave. These are, for the most part, service organisations like police forces, health authorities, airlines and so on. A common characteristic of such organisations is that it is the most junior staff who have the most contact with the outside world and are therefore largely responsible for establishing how the organisation as a whole is perceived.

In any police force much the most significant factor in both identity and image is the behaviour in face to face encounters of individual police officers with their publics. Even in organisations where other factors are important – eg banks and airlines – behaviour may remain a significant factor in identity.

The dominant factor

In most organisations it is a combination of product/service, environment, communication and behaviour that comes together in various proportions to form the identity. However, the balance between these four factors is rarely equal and a priority early on in any identity programme is to determine which predominates.

Press advertising for Benetton. A dramatic campaign to make the public aware of the company behind the brand.

The central idea/vision

The fundamental idea behind an identity programme is that in everything the organisation does, everything it owns, and everything it produces it should project a clear idea of what it is and what its aims are. The most significant way in which this can be done is by making everything in and around the organisation – its products, buildings, communications and behaviour – consistent in purpose and performance and, where this is appropriate, in appearance too.

Outward consistency of this kind will only be achieved, and for that matter is only appropriate, if it is the manifestation of an inward consistency – a consistency of purpose. This consistency of purpose derives from the vision or the central idea and is almost always the base from which a successful identity programme can be developed.

The central idea or the vision is the force that drives the organisation. It is what the organisation is about, what it stands for, what it believes in.

Quite often the organisation involved in developing a new identity is more concerned about what it can become than about what it is. In this sense the vision is created by ambitions formed from the central idea. But the vision must be unique. All organisations are unique even if the products/services that they make/sell are more or less the same as those of their competitors. It is their history, their structure, their strategy, the personalities who have created and dominated them, their successes and their failures, that shape them and make the organisation what it is.

Most organisations are not naturally especially conscious or thoughtful about these matters. If they have a central idea it is implicitly enshrined in the way they get on with their business. Such identities are often characterised by their informality. The company's behaviour patterns, its communications and the appearance of its products, services, offices and showrooms, are a result of the unconscious influence of a few powerful individuals. They grow

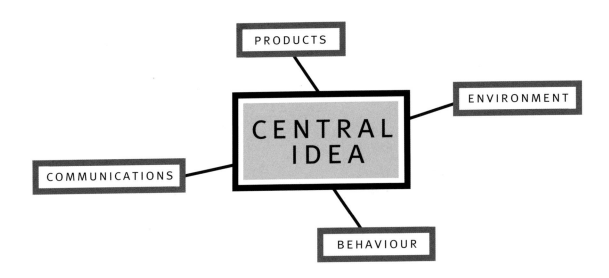

As the communist régimes collapsed all over Central and Eastern Europe the symbols of oppression were overthrown with them. Shown here Stalin's statue falling in Albania.

and the appearance of its products, services, offices and showrooms, are a result of the unconscious influence of a few powerful individuals. They grow up dominated more often than not by the personality of their founder.

But there always comes a time in a successful organisation when the informal, intuitive, perhaps muddled, but shared vision or central idea has to be formalised, clarified and made coherent. And that is when the explicit, institutionalised, self-aware identity programme is introduced.

The symbol

The symbol, or as it is increasingly and often incorrectly called, the logo, usually lies at the heart of an identity programme. Its prime purpose is to present the central idea of the organisation with impact, brevity and immediacy. The symbol encapsulates the identity.

Symbols are immensely powerful. They act as visual triggers which work many times faster and more explosively than words to set off a train of ideas in the mind. Many symbols are, as we know from Jung and others, an intrinsic part of the human vocabulary of expression and comprehension. Symbols can unleash the most complex and profound emotions.

When the communist régimes of Eastern Europe tottered and fell in the late 80s, the first action the liberated peoples of each country took to celebrate their freedom from tyranny was publicly to topple the symbolism of oppression. We saw on our television screens how they threw down the statues of Lenin and Stalin, and how they cut out with scissors the hammer and sickle from their national flags.

No wonder then that the symbol is almost always the focal point from which the identity is judged. As people involved in the identity activity we may feel that to judge a whole identity programme on its symbolism trivialises and distorts what we do, that it ignores all the other aspects of our work, but we have to understand that in working with symbols we are engaged with profound forces – some of which are half buried within our subconscious – which have the ability to provoke remarkable emotion.

Much of the criticism of identity work is based around the idea that in creating symbols the client and its consultants are attempting to manipulate and control its various audiences in an Orwellian fashion. The truth is rather more complex. By bringing the organisation into focus, the identity inevitably subjects it to close scrutiny. Where the organisation lives up to the standards it proclaims, this scrutiny is favourable; where it doesn't, the results are dire. In this context then, identity is not about making poor organisations look good but about distinguishing organisations from each other.

Symbols represent the never-ending human search to reach into the subconscious: the Christian cross, the Aids symbol, St George and the Dragon, in this version by Ucello (c. 1460) symbolising the battle for the human spirit between Good and Evil, and the Bovis humming bird all mine the same rich vein.

Who it's aimed at

The internal/external focus

Identity is a most unusual resource. When it is used with its maximum impact and inspired from the top, it has an influence on all parts of the organisation: design, marketing, selling, purchasing, recruitment, finance and so on. It also influences legislators, stockbrokers and financial analysts, journalists and other kinds of opinion formers. This capability to encompass both the internal and external worlds can be a source of strength, because it brings with it cohesion, coherence and clarity.

However, when identity is not a main board initiative things can be different. Some managers are uncomfortable operating with such an overarching concept. They like to use a resource exclusively within their own part of the organisation. Identity, therefore, is sometimes hijacked by one division or another, either by marketing, by communication, or by human resource people and employed by them exclusively.

Of course it does sometimes happen that an identity programme is deliberately aimed either at an external or internal audience by top management. Sometimes identity programmes are either internally focused, that is aimed largely at the internal audiences of the organisation, employees around the world at various levels and so on, or externally focused, that is aimed largely at the outside world, at customers, or shareholders or the financial community.

These two kinds of identity programme have somewhat different aims and objectives and use rather different but overlapping tools to achieve their purpose.

The externally focused identity – corporate branding

This can also be described as the marketing focused identity or, more fashionably, corporate branding. Its purpose is to differentiate the organisation, or part of the organisation, and its products and services from those of its competitors in the minds primarily of customers and potential customers, but also in the minds of financial audiences, opinion formers, journalists and other target audiences.

Here the identity programme works to create and establish the corporate product, service or retail brand through names, visual symbols, packaging, environments and so on. In this context identity is part of the marketing process and in this kind of programme close co-operation with advertising agencies, product development consultants and other specialists is required.

The internally focused identity – vision programme

This can also be described as the vision focused identity. Its purpose, often at a time of crisis, change of direction or restructuring, is to create in the minds of all employees, at all levels, in all divisions, everywhere, a clear idea of what the organisation is and what it stands for.

Here the identity programme seeks to create and launch a vision based around a central determining theme. In this type of identity activity, which is often largely to do with the announcement, introduction and management of organisational and

behavioural change, the disciplines with which consultants work will be geared towards human resources. Name, graphics, environments and other design disciplines will of course play a major role as part of the change process, and identity consultants will act as partners in the communication of ideas around the behaviour programme.

Target audiences

Although many identity programmes are either marketing led (external) or vision led (internal), there will almost always be an overlap between them. Corporate branding, largely an external issue, inevitably has some internal impact too and a vision programme can be a vehicle which presents the corporate aim to the outside world. Pensioners, shareholders and journalists may also be customers. Customers may also be shareholders, or want to be, and so on.

A list of the main audience groups will be found in Appendix C.

Different audiences will form a view of an organisation based on the totality of the impressions that it makes on them. Where these impressions are contradictory – where impressions made in one place are different from those made somewhere else – the overall impression will be negative, or at any rate confusing. In a world which is increasingly transparent and open, it is no longer possible for the corporation to hide behind its brands, as Unilever's Persil fiasco of 1994 so clearly demonstrates.

It is also clear that if the organisation makes a

public relations blunder in one part of the world, repercussions will be felt elsewhere. Shell's experience in 1995 with its proposed disposal of the Brent Spar platform, surely emphasises this point. This means that the best and most successful identity programmes will be both internally and externally focused and that they will be both coherent and effectively co-ordinated.

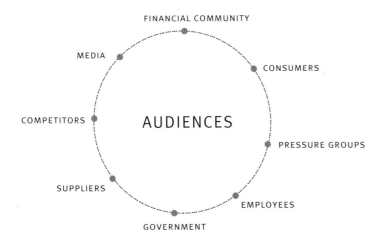

FINANCIAL COMMUNITY

MEDIA

CONSUMERS

COMPETITORS

AUDIENCES

PRESSURE GROUPS

SUPPLIERS

EMPLOYEES

GOVERNMENT

The audiences of the organisation overlap and interrelate. Customers may also be shareholders and take an active part in pressure groups (Shell's Brent Spar fiasco 1995). Competitors may be partners and suppliers, or even all three simultaneously (Airbus Industrie).

Identity structures

There are three types of identity structure: monolithic, endorsed and branded. This diagram shows them.

Structures

Every organisation needs to consider its identity in the light of its structure. The identity structure should be clear, easy to comprehend and it should make the organisation's strategy visible both internally and externally.

The identities of most organisations which have given consideration to the matter fall broadly into one of three categories.

These categories are not mutually exclusive and rigidly defined. There is some overlap. Some exist because of powerful and venerable traditions, eg consumer goods companies traditionally have branded identities, while banks traditionally have monolithic identities. In terms of creating and sustaining one idea about the organisation, the monolithic structure is the easiest to handle and the branded structure the most difficult, but fundamentally the identity structure is dictated by the external rather than the internal requirement.

Monolithic

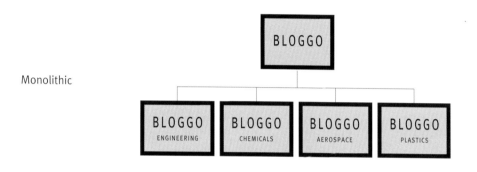

Endorsed

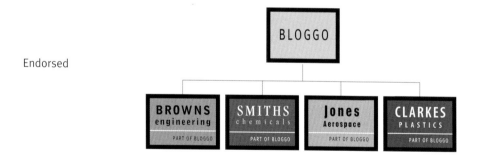

Branded

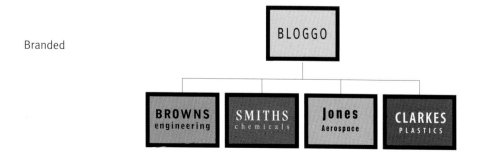

Each of these categories has advantages and disadvantages. None is intrinsically superior to any of the others. Each is appropriate in different circumstances. When circumstances change it may sometimes be appropriate to change or modify identity structures.

Monolithic – the single business identity

The organisation uses one name and one visual system throughout (eg Yamaha, BP, Virgin).

Endorsed – the multi-business identity

The companies forming a group are perceived either by visual or written endorsement to be part of that group (eg Nestlé, United Technologies, Forte).

Branded – the brand-based identity

The company operates through a series of brands or companies which are apparently unrelated, both to one another and to the corporation (eg GrandMet, Unilever, Procter & Gamble).

Monolithic – the single business identity

Companies operating a monolithic identity quite deliberately use their corporate name to promote a special idea about themselves. Sometimes the name operates in a single market place or a few which are linked by technology (BP). At its most effective, however, the monolithic identity covers a broad spectrum of activities.

Perhaps the most striking example of an organisation which uses a monolithic identity system to best advantage is Richard Branson's Virgin, whose name and identity, stemming from the original music business, now embrace amongst other things an airline, a cola and financial services. For many people evidently Virgin is not only a seal of quality, but a symbol of a way of life.

- The fundamental strength of the monolithic identity is that because each product and service launched by the organisation has the same name, style and character as all the others, everything within the organisation by way of promotion or product supports everything else. Relations with staff, suppliers and the outside world are clear, consistent, relatively easy to control and usually economical to manage.
- Companies with monolithic identities tend as a consequence to have high visibility and a clear positioning which can be a great advantage in the market place.

virgin atlantic

 direct
personal financial service

Virgin has the ultimate monolithic identity. The Virgin name is currently (1995) used on an airline, financial services, a vodka and a cola amongst other things, as well as on the original music businesses. It would work equally well on clothes, food and a dozen other activities provided that each of them fitted the Virgin image.

Endorsed – the multi-business identity

Since a large number of companies have grown primarily by acquisition and seek to employ the endorsed identity system, this is perhaps the most significant category, at least numerically. United Technologies, Forte, P&O and Nestlé all employ variations of an endorsed identity system.

Companies which project an endorsed identity normally have the following characteristics:

- They have grown largely by acquisition. Often they have acquired competitors, suppliers and customers, each with its own name, culture, tradition and reputation amongst its own network of audiences.
- They are multi-sector businesses, operating in a wide band of activities – manufacturing, wholesaling, retailing, selling components to competitors, making finished products them-selves and so on.
- They are concerned to retain the goodwill associated with the brands and companies which they have acquired, but at the same time they want to superimpose their own management style, reward systems, attitudes and sometimes name upon their subsidiaries.
- They have certain audiences, such as the financial world, opinion formers, possibly some suppliers and customers and so on, whom they want to impress with their total size and strength. Among these they want to emphasise uniformity and consistency as opposed to diversity.

Nestlé

Nestlé endorses many of its brands including relatively recent acquisitions like Rolo, Kit-Kat and Lyons Maid. However, Nestlé is selective. Perrier, also a Nestlé brand, does not carry the endorsement.

- They have sometimes acquired competitive ranges of products. They therefore have problems of competition, even confusion, among suppliers, customers and often their own employees.
- They frequently operate in many different countries in which their products and their reputations vary.

Companies seeking to create an identity covering a wide range of activities, with subsidiaries that have differing and frequently competitive backgrounds, face a complicated task. On the one hand, certainly at the corporate level and for corporate audiences, they want to create the clear idea of a single, but multi-faceted organisation that has a sense of purpose. On the other hand, they want to allow the identities of the numerous companies and brands they have acquired to continue to flourish in order to retain goodwill, both in the market place and among employees.

This requires a very difficult balancing act. These aims cannot, without the greatest possible sensitivity, be achieved simultaneously.

Branded – the brand-based identity

Some companies, for the most part those in pharmaceuticals, food, drink and other fast-moving consumer goods, sometimes separate their identities as corporations from those of the brands which they make and sell (eg Procter & Gamble, Unilever and GrandMet). At the corporate level these companies reach out to all of the audiences of the monolithic or endorsed

United Distillers, itself part of Guinness, owns most of the great names in Scotch whisky as well as many famous names in other spirits. Its success has been to emphasise the individual personalities of each of its brands and to extend brand families. Shown here – a small selection of brands and Johnnie Walker Red Label and Black Label, part of an extended Johnnie Walker family.

company, but they do not present their corporate face to the consumer. So far as the final customer is concerned the corporation does not exist. What the customer perceives is only the brand. The reasons why some companies pursue this policy are:

- The long-standing tradition of the fast-moving consumer goods industry is that the consumer is readily influenced by basic and obvious symbolism (eg Wash'n Go = clean, fast and youthful, Poison = sophisticated, Flora = healthy). This somewhat naive symbolism might seem to be inappropriate for a global, complex corporation.
- Brands may have a life cycle of their own, quite distinct from that of the company.
- Brands from the same company may well compete in the market place and their integrity might appear to be damaged in the eyes of the consumer if they were known to come from the same stable.
- Brands should be free to develop powerful identities of their own, appropriate to their consumers.

An identity for a subsidiary or a holding

Throughout this section, and indeed elsewhere in this Guide, it has been assumed that identity should embrace the totality of the organisation. While this is often the case, it frequently happens that divisions or semi-autonomous subsidiaries of corporations may feel the need for separate identity programmes. This is particularly true of corporate branding where a new service (eg BA's Club Europe) is based around the identity of the corporate whole.

Sometimes the reverse situation operates and the holding wishes, for sound commercial reasons, to separate itself from one or all of its subsidiaries (eg Kingfisher). This situation occurs particularly among companies with endorsed or branded identities.

In developing these programmes it is essential to get agreement from and work with the corporate body, so that the modulations of the basic identity required by the new corporate brand are acceptable.

Until 1989 Woolworths was the name both of the holding company and one of its trading subsidiaries. Because this caused confusion amongst financial audiences in particular, Wolff Olins was commissioned to create a new name and visual identity for the holding – now called Kingfisher.

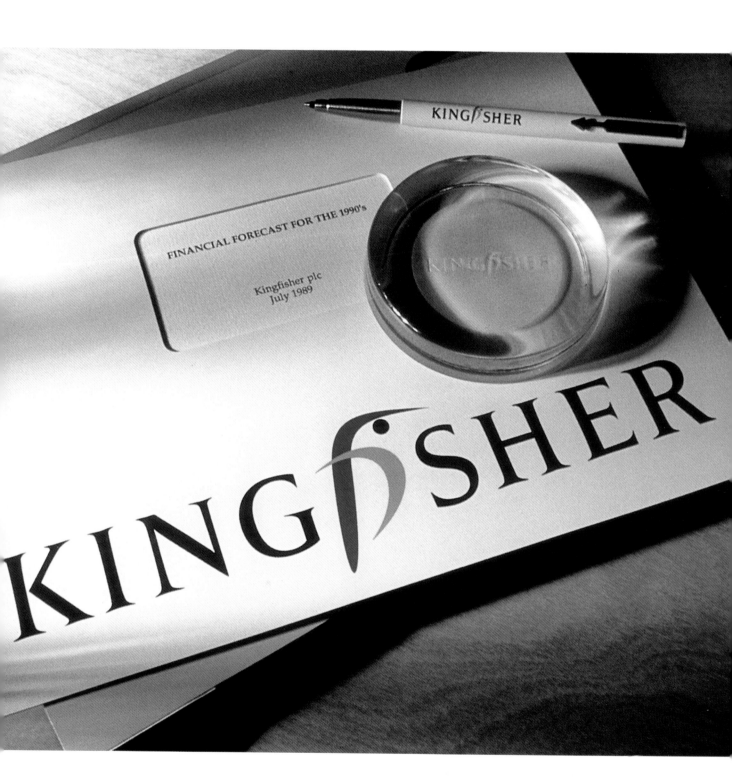

Why and when to introduce it

A climate of change

Change comes from three principal directions for the corporation – globalisation, competition and mergers. In each case identity plays a major part in helping the organisation adjust to a new environment.

Globalisation

Since the 1970s the pace at which corporations have globalised – that is to say, have treated the world as their market place for designing, purchasing and manufacturing, as well as marketing and selling – has massively increased. We all expect large organisations to operate globally – Sony, MacDonalds and VW are household names all over the world – but it is increasingly the case that much smaller companies with much more specialised reputations are going global too. In pharmaceuticals, for example, it isn't only the giants like SmithKline Beecham, Glaxo Wellcome and Boehringer Ingelheim that are global. Comparatively small and specialised organisations like Lundbeck in Denmark and Amersham International of the UK are global players too. If such organisations are to succeed they have to adapt to diverse national and regional cultures.

How globalisation affects the corporate strategy and structure

Corporations with global aspirations or activities may find it appropriate to organise themselves around the product sector rather than the nation. Ford is a leading exponent of this principle. Shell,

one of the largest, most successful and oldest of
global organisations, announced a significant
change in this direction in April 1995.

The structural reorganisation which the
globalisation process demands leads inexorably
to a new vision for the corporation. If this vision
is to be understood and accepted worldwide it will
lead to large-scale behavioural change programmes
and these are sometimes accompanied by major
identity changes. In this context then the change
of identity becomes part of organisational and
behavioural change.

Competition

It is becoming increasingly evident that the nature
of competition is changing. It was once possible to
choose between competing products and services

on the basis of price, quality or service – rational
or quasi-rational factors. Today in most activities
that is no longer possible.

Look at financial services, petrol retailing, airlines
and the chemical industry, just to take some broad
industrial and commercial areas at random. In all of
these activities there is very little or no real
difference between the products and services of
the leading players in terms of price, quality and
service. Being as good as the best of the competition
is now sufficient only to enable an organisation to
stay in the race.

In these situations emotional factors, being liked,
admired or respected more than the competition,
help the organisation to win. And that is why so
many organisations now invest so heavily in what
is increasingly being called corporate branding.

BT, now one of the world's leading telecoms companies, is a classic case history of identity used as a change management resource. The combined external pressures of privatisation, globalisation and competition, together with astonishing leaps in technology, created the opportunity, for change. The new identity by Wolff Olins – shown here – was a significant input into the change management process. All this has made the organisation unrecognisably different from the old British Telecom.

Mergers, takeovers, alliances and privatisations

In real life mergers rarely happen; whenever one company joins up with another, one of them almost always comes out on top. In this situation it is vital to bury past animosities and make a new beginning with an entirely new behavioural pattern, name and visual identity. Here the behavioural and visual manifestations of the identity process have to work together in creating and managing change, so that when the new organisation emerges employees no longer continually evoke the past or refer to their colleagues from a different background as members of the rival gang, but operate so far as this is possible given the constraints of human nature, in a positive fashion. Hence the long recognised need for the identity discipline in mergers.

There are, however, two rather more recent variations on the merger theme. The first is the organisation formed from traditional rivals to produce a particular product or service for a limited period of time, or with a limited objective – this is often called the strategic alliance. The European Airbus project now transmuted into a permanent and apparently viable organisation was originally conceived on these lines – and there are many more.

And the second is the privatised corporation. Since the initial wave of Thatcher privatisations in Britain in the early 80s this is a phenomenon which has spread all over the world. In both the strategic alliance and the privatised corporation a new way of looking, feeling and behaving is vital to help the new organisation effectively to emerge from its public sector predecessor.

The trigger for change

These three factors, globalisation, competition and change of status, lie behind most identity programmes. But there is almost always a trigger which sets the change going. This may be the arrival of a new chief executive, evidence of too much internal competition, an indication that the outside world misunderstands and undervalues the organisation, and so on.

The brief

Identity programmes, as I have already indicated, usually emerge as the result of outside events impacting on the organisation. The situations that derive from these events demand action. Either immediately or soon, something has to be done. Corporate management makes a judgement and prepares a brief for action.

Merger – two Finnish banks

When the two major Finnish banks, UBF and KOP, merged in 1995 to form Merita, one of the largest banks in the European Nordic region, the new management needed to create a single organisation with a single behaviour pattern, a single purpose, a single name and of course a single visual identity. This was a classic merger of competitors.

In such a case the brief will, in principle, cover both internal and external aspects of identity. And deriving from this, it will set new boundaries, objectives and targets for the new, larger and more ambitious organisation. It will take into account issues such as name, symbol, branch design, signage – all external issues. It will also take into account the creation of a new single behaviour pattern which bonds historical rivals – an internal issue.

Competition – the petrol station forecourt war

Shell's retail service station network was relaunched in the early 1990s largely because its main competitors, Exxon, Texaco, BP and other players like Repsol and Q8 had upgraded their service station network and focused on selling food and other profitable products through shops, and Shell did not want to be left behind. In addition Shell, like the other petrol retailers, wanted to hit back at the supermarket chains which were eating into their traditional petrol retailing business. Shell's retail service station network is a high profile public manifestation of the whole organisation – the programme has therefore had an impact upon the image of Shell worldwide.

This example is typical of an identity programme commissioned because of fierce competition in the market place – an attempt to increase market share, or stop decline. Such an identity programme will probably be more external than internal in its focus and will rely largely on marketing and communication tools. This is classic corporate branding.

As supermarkets and petrol retailers encroach remorselessly on each other's territory, competition between them intensifies. Shown here, three retailers in the UK battling head to head (1995) in a struggle largely influenced by identity.

New product/service – the mobile telecoms battle

Identity programmes may be created because a new service arrives in the market place. In the world of mobile telecoms there has been an explosion of new entrants over the past few years. Orange, the mobile phone network from Hutchison Communications, is one of the main players. It needed to create a new name, identity and positioning to establish itself as a viable player.

This is also an example of corporate branding.

Vision – a German pharmaceutical company goes global

Boehringer Ingelheim, the giant German-based pharmaceutical company, needed to become more global and decentralised in its outlook, behaviour pattern and personality. It launched a vision programme aimed at its employees throughout the world. The vision was based around the self-evident truth that the company was innovation led. Boehringer Ingelheim's staff see the organisation in a new light as a result of this programme.

This is an example of an identity programme which is largely vision focused and internally directed.

Talk.

The Orange Talk Awards

listen.

the
future's
bright...

US

A world of change...

The most important element of our organisation is our people.
Every one has a role to play and there are several challenges in
our future. We want to hear your ideas for making us meet the
future we should be all of us.

We are committed to ensuring that we have the highest standards.
A secure business that runs on its own power. To be allowed we want all of
our staff to be involved in their field. This is the chance you've built to us
make them. If we want our standards through a simple thing you can make
them a strong business in a shorter company to work for.

We will succeed if we share both a share a vision from.
It won't all happen overnight, but if we all work
together it **will** happen.

The success of our company will depend upon our team working
together, reviewing the employee and software to understand
wireless communications, delivering the future.

our new
brand

the first real consumer brand

I use an Apple
I work for Shell
I drive a Caterpillar

thank you

our vision

the wirefree world; choice and control

Identity as a corporate resource

A corporate resource

If it is effectively introduced and sustained, identity will become a major management resource. Like finance, investment, personnel, research and development, marketing, information technology and so on, identity needs an appropriate power base, disciplines, adequate funding, commitment and management. If the identity resource receives this backing it will operate just as effectively and give much the same return as any other corporate resource – if it doesn't it will wither on the vine.

The importance and potential influence of an identity management system can be best understood by examining two other systems already functioning in the organisation – financial management and information technology management.

The role models

Financial management

It is impossible to run any kind of organisation without properly co-ordinated financial controls and the appropriate systems. The corporate financial system is seen as legitimate throughout every part of the organisation. In some global organisations it is the financial management system together with the information system which provide the glue that holds the corporation together.

Financial management, with all its dedicated staff, its annual, monthly and even weekly rites of forecasting, budgeting, targeting and so on, is accepted unquestioningly as part of corporate life.

Information systems management

Information systems management is now as vital to the corporation as financial management. Over the past decades it has first invaded·and then integrated itself into every corner of organisational life. An entire function has developed around assessing, satisfying and managing the organisation's information needs. In fact information systems have become so sophisticated and complex that they have come to dominate the actions, behaviour and structure of many of the organisations in which they are used. In banking and other financial service organisations it is at least arguable that information systems are the dominant function and largely determine the way the company does its business.

Identity management

Identity management should be put into the same perspective as financial management or information systems management – that is, as a corporate resource which will work effectively when it embraces every part of the organisation. Every department of the organisation, from marketing to purchasing to human resources, should incorporate identity management into its thinking, behaviour patterns and actions. Only if an organisation takes its identity management as seriously as this will it achieve its maximum potential. Examples of organisations which take their identity management really seriously and are reaping rewards for it are

referred to in Section Seven, Stage Four, Implementation – making it happen.

Some organisations already have influential design management structures from which identity management systems can be developed. Information technology can be a considerable help here as multi-media techniques and electronic manuals of various kinds bring the identity resource into the heart of the organisation.

Consultants

The need for professional help

Organisations are rarely sufficiently objective, self-aware or experienced in the appropriate disciplines to carry out an identity programme without external assistance, so they will usually look to outside consultants for professional help.

Because the identity field is both expanding and mutating, it is beginning to embrace a wide range of disciplines. Now more than ever before it is important to pick a consultant with care.

Traditionally identity has been the province of design consultants.

The field is now broadening. Consultants in identity vary a good deal, for reasons which I have explained in the Introduction to this Guide. Some have a characteristic visual style and concentrate on design rather than analysis. These consultancies employ only graphic designers and project managers of various kinds. A few consultancies have built up their businesses around identity work or are specialists in this field, others offer a wide range of services from design of different kinds to change management. Some are familiar with large multinational companies and others are not. Their size varies from those with 100+ staff to one-man bands. The range of choice is wide; so is the range of fees.

Consultants should be appointed on the basis of their track record, their personality, their comprehension of the problem, their range of disciplines, their presentations, their proposed working methods and, of course, on whether the personal chemistry between them and the client works.

Partnerships

Because the identity activity overlaps with so many other disciplines – marketing, communication, human resources, design and so on – it may sometimes be appropriate to appoint two specialist consultancies working in tandem, say a behavioural change consultancy and a design consultancy. Sometimes the best way to handle the programme is to work with a group of consultants: a strategic consultancy, an identity consultancy, a behavioural change consultancy and an advertising agency. In this case, in order to avoid too much jostling for position, it might be useful to appoint one of these as prime contractor.

Although advertising agencies and PR companies can make a contribution at appropriate stages in the process, they are not, and for the most part do not purport to be, main contractors in this kind of work. Their value, both as advisers and practitioners, emerges when the corporate identity programme has been launched. At that point there is often a need for corporate advertising and internal/external communication work to complement and reinforce the identity effort.

In the UK a variety of trade bodies can provide a list of consultancies. (See Appendix D for their addresses.) In other countries similar trade bodies should be consulted. Advertising agencies and PR consultancies and other professional advisers can also be consulted for names where appropriate. The best recommendation, however, comes from those who have already successfully used the consultancy service.

The identities of
Prudential and P&O
(both by Wolff Olins) are
used with power,
consistency, subtlety
and humour in
press and TV advertising
campaigns.

Starting up & managing the programme

Preliminaries

Large-scale identity programmes are commissioned relatively rarely. The organisation committing itself to an identity programme for the first time, therefore, may not always be fully aware of its implications. There is not necessarily a requirement to make a massive commitment. It may be easier for some companies to enter into the process on a step-by-step basis. Sometimes one part of an organisation may commission an identity project. The issues involved here are referred to in Section Three.

It is very important for Chairmen or Chief Executives to have a clear idea of what they want to achieve in the longer term. Is it a complete corporate turnround? Is it to re-invigorate, re-inspire and create more cohesion internally? Is it to project a clearer series of ideas about the organisation externally? Is it to push up the share price, or some similar tactical objective? Do they want to start with a specific job – something that has to be done – and possibly move on from there? Do they want some modification and modulation of what currently exists? Or are there other factors involved? Whichever is the case it is usually appropriate to tap in to the tested methodology of the identity activity.

Two levels of control

Let us assume for the purposes of this Guide that the programme will be a major operation. In this case it is run from the top and managed from the middle levels of the organisation. Without overt commitment from the top, the programme may not get properly off the ground. It certainly won't become a viable management resource. But it also needs tight middle management control; without this, it may flounder and sink without trace.

When an identity programme has been decided upon the Chairman or Chief Executive should appoint an executive to manage it who will directly report to him. Such a person will often have a design, communication, marketing or human resources background. It's helpful if he/she has had some experience of the identity process.

Because of the varying nature of identity work it is essential to clarify the brief and sort out the team as early as possible. For example, the creation, launching and implementation of a corporate branding programme demands different skills, disciplines and methodologies and therefore, to some degree, a different team from that for an internal change programme.

Working party and steering group

The identity manager's first job, then, is to form a small working party which runs the programme. This working party should normally consist of representatives from marketing, design, communications and human resources and possibly other activities on the client's side, together with the consultancy team. This working party should report to a smaller steering group headed by the Chairman or Chief Executive.

The stages of work

The basic building blocks of an identity programme are as follows:

- Stage One
  Investigation, analysis and strategic recommendations

- Stage Two
  Developing the identity

- Stage Three
  Launch and introduction – communicating the vision

- Stage Four
  Implementation – making it happen

These stages assume that the programme starts at the beginning, goes on to the middle and finishes at the end. As identity work becomes more complex and sophisticated this may not happen. Parts of the programme may be left out, new parts introduced – and so on. The pattern outlined in the pages that follow should therefore be treated only as a guide.

Investigation, analysis and strategic recommendations

This stage consists of an interview programme, a series of audits and appropriate desk research.

These are the overall issues which should be addressed:

- Nature of the industry/sector in which the organisation operates

  Industry/sector size, growth patterns, rates of change, competitiveness, use of technology, environmental concerns, corporate culture, and profitability.

- The organisation itself and its characteristics

  First: size, position, profitability, market share, competitiveness, quality, advertising and environmental responsibility.

  Second: perceptions about the organisation's personality, core values, central idea and vision.

- Brands, businesses and divisions

  How the different brands, products and services of the organisation and its totality are seen and understood by its different audiences. What each part of the business thinks about all the other parts and the centre.

Desk research

The desk research involves looking at the organisation's history and structure: how it grew, who were the influential personalities and what were the significant events in its history.

Interview programme

The interviews are intended, first, to gain insights and determine to what extent there is a consensus about the organisation and second, to uncover the issues that both unite and divide it.

The interviews embrace individuals representing different points of view, both inside and outside the organisation. Interviews are normally, but not always, carried out by the identity consultants. The number of interviews will vary according to the size and complexity of the organisation, from a minimum of 10–20 up to 100+. The number depends upon the complexity of audiences to be interviewed.

Internal interviews

The interview programme is not intended to be statistically significant but it should be representative. Interviewees should be selected from all levels and all parts of the company. They should reasonably represent the age/sex profile of the organisation.

The programme starts with a brief note from the Chairman or Chief Executive to all internal interviewees saying that some research is being undertaken on the organisation's identity and guaranteeing confidentiality for the interviews.

Interviews should be informal, confidential, and loosely structured. Although interviewers must be clear about the issues they should not follow a set questionnaire. The tone of the meeting should be cordial and informal.

The responses of internal interviewees will be conditioned by their role, responsibilities, and length of service.

Each internal group will have a view of its own significance and of the competence, loyalty and roles of the other divisions, brands and services of the corporation. All the divisions will have a view of the centre. These views are sometimes highly critical.

On the issue of name and visual style, people from some divisions or countries may say that controlling their own name and image is vital to success in their markets.

Respondents quite often find it hard to discuss abstract issues like vision. They are more likely to respond to questions on morale, leadership and clarity of purpose.

People at the centre normally have their own perspective on the loyalty, ability and significance of each division. Newer acquisitions will express different views from older businesses. Nationals of the 'home country' of the company will have different views from overseas operations. And so on. It's a rich field.

External interviews

External interviews should be conducted with suppliers, customers, competitors, collaborators, journalists and, where appropriate, representatives from other groups like government and trade associations. Interviewees must be selected to ensure a representative sample.

The purpose of these interviews is to find out how much outsiders know both about the mechanics of the company (size, profitability, ownership and its products, services and organisation skills), what their views are about its strengths, weaknesses and impact on the outside world and what image, attitudes and overall perceptions they have about the organisation.

Interviewees should be given only the most general idea of the purpose of the interview. Sometimes it even helps not to reveal the purpose of the interview. It pays to be oblique.

External interviews are useful in different ways from internal interviews. Often they reveal much about what outsiders don't know about an organisation. Sometimes outsiders know an organisation very well. Generally though, people outside a company have a partial and distorted view of it. They often know very little about its products or geographical spread. This does not of course inhibit them from expressing quite emphatic views.

Even in the financial world, where analysts are paid to dissect a company's structure and performance, there is often a great deal of misunderstanding and misinformation. But even a distorted picture reveals a great deal. Remember we are specifically looking for perceptions.

It is the combination of internal and external interviews that so often gives such an interesting picture.

The audits

Then there are the three audits, for communications, behaviour and design. Emphasis will be placed on each according to their significance within the whole programme and upon whether the programme as a whole is internally or externally directed – or both.

The communications audit

The communications audit examines what the organisation says, to whom and how, and whether it uses a consistent tone of voice. It also examines whether the organisation listens: to its own people, and to outsiders; to dealers, suppliers, investors and customers.

Areas to examine are:

- how the communication system works
- the links (if any) between internal and external communications
- the context and quality of external and internal communications
- who says what to whom and how
- how the organisation communicates with its employees and, where appropriate, with other quasi-internal organisations (although this is partly a behavioural issue)
- is there a consistent tone in which the organisation communicates?

At the same time as it looks at its internal communications, the audit team should consider how the organisation deals with its external audiences through press and public relations, annual reports, display and TV advertising, and other formal and informal channels.

As part of the audit process, the technical and general media should be reviewed in order to see how the group and its activities are perceived.

An audit of this kind is particularly important in an organisation comprising a large number of smallish units, like a bank with its widespread branch network, or an automobile manufacturer with a network of independently owned dealers. In this situation what people in the various units are told, about what is going on and when, directly affects what they feel about the organisation.

The behavioural audit

Much of the feedback regarding the way in which people within a company interact both with each other and with the various external groups with whom they deal, can be derived from the interview programme and the other audits, but in many cases a specific audit on corporate attitudes will be required.

Here are some issues to consider:

- Does the company invest in the development of people – other than in their performance?
- Does it set personal performance objectives and does it appraise performance regularly?
- Does it reward people in relation to their performance?

- Is there a genuine commitment to service, value, and long-term relationships or merely lip-service?
- Is it trustworthy in honouring its commitments?
- Is it a good neighbour?
- Does it manifest any principles not directly relevant to business?

Questions on this topic are intended to reveal fundamental attitudes.

Sometimes the audit team may have access to customer opinion/satisfaction research, in which case a parallel set of questions can deal with the way the organisation is seen to behave:

- What are the different parts of the organisation like to deal with?
- How helpful are staff in answering questions and resolving problems?
- How quickly are customers served or telephone calls answered?
- Are its representatives polite or rude?

In a service activity like a police force or airline, behaviour is an important factor and this audit must be given appropriate weight.

The design or visual audit

The primary purpose of this audit is to examine the way in which the different parts of the organisation present themselves in terms of their physical output: graphics, products and environments. An example of everything that the organisation produces must be collected and examined for consistency, coherence and cost. At the same time, the team should photograph and, if necessary, visit a representative example of the different buildings, sites, showrooms, stores and offices which the organisation occupies.

When senior management examines examples of the totality of the corporate output with all its inevitable inconsistencies and contradictions it usually has a salutary and disturbing impact and reinforces the need for coherence.

Findings

When all audits and interviews have been carried out the working party meets to consider the findings. From the findings it is of course necessary to develop a series of recommendations – for the board to consider and act upon.

These recommendations will be based around the requirements of the programme. They must be relevant to the issues that have been investigated, they must be clear and if necessary they may be radical.

Working party meetings should have taken place regularly on a formal basis, say once a month, and informally more frequently. During these meetings the detailed recommendations will have been thrashed out. After discussion, the findings and recommendations are formally presented to the smaller steering group and then the board. This process can take between two and four months depending on the size of the organisation and the scope of the interview/audit programme. The outside consultancy almost always prepares and makes the presentation.

The presentation

It is important to take into account that identity is likely to be an unfamiliar, even alien, subject to many of the board members to whom the consultants will present and they should therefore take care to make their presentation clear, logical, relevant and comprehensive.

A presentation of findings should start by recalling the brief: 'This is what we were asked to do'. It should go on to describe what the team did. Then what they found. And then: 'This is the action that we recommend'. In this way the consultancy can explain in a step-by-step fashion how it has arrived at its conclusions. It can justify and explain what it thinks should be done next.

The salient issues must be explained clearly, succinctly and with ample evidence. Suppose that a large world-wide organisation which has grown by acquisition and has a plethora of companies, each with its own ethos, product and presentation engaged in different activities, is under scrutiny. And suppose further that the organisation is perceived internally to be unco-ordinated, lacking a clear sense of direction, with overlapping and unclear lines of responsibility, with no clear personnel policy and products of varying quality. Suppose, in other words, that it is perceived internally as a bit of a shapeless mess.

The likelihood is that external audiences will reflect a similar picture. They will only know bits of the organisation, its size and scale will be under-rated and its reputation will vary dramatically according to the part that people know – and so on.

If this is how the organisation is perceived, then this perception, however unpalatable, has to be clearly laid out and backed by appropriate evidence both from the interviews and the audits and desk research.

Recommendations

Findings – in other words how the organisation is perceived – and why it is perceived that way – must be accompanied by recommendations for action.

What we should do about it – the central idea/vision

During the course of the investigation, the special characteristics of the organisation, those characteristics that make it unique, should have emerged. Equally the opportunities for the organisation, its ambitions, or the ambitions of many of its leading personalities, will have been explored. In addition marketing opportunities and the positioning which the organisation might adopt will have to be taken into account.

This is the opportunity for the organisation to play to its strengths: to develop a central idea which reveals its personality and a vision which emphasises its sense of purpose and which helps it to seize the marketing high ground.

This central idea must be put forward at the presentation, discussed in detail, where necessary modified, further discussed and ultimately agreed and encapsulated in writing.

One side of A4 paper should normally be quite enough to outline what the company is, what it does, how it does it and what its vision for its future is. This brief document must avoid clichés, get to the heart of the matter and outline a concept which is both unique to the organisation and recognised as realistic by those who work for and deal with it.

This central idea/vision must form the basis from which the whole identity programme is developed. It is vital to the whole operation to get it right and then to get it agreed and signed.

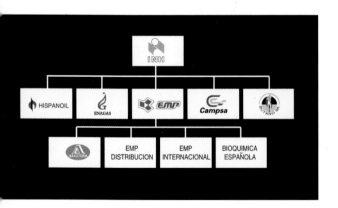

INH – the huge and clumsy state organisation from which Repsol emerged.

Repsol is Spain's largest, most admired and most successful company. Its identity (by Wolff Olins) as the Spanish player in the major international oil company league is based around a clear vision.

Following from the development of and agreement to the vision/central idea, the second stage of work can begin.

Example – Repsol: an identity based on a vision

When the Spanish oil company Repsol was formed in the 1980s from the autarchic, state monopoly Istituto Nacional Hydrocarburos, which constituted virtually the entire Spanish energy sector, the central idea/vision emerged naturally from the new positioning. Spain had just entered the European Union, and the world's major oil companies had the opportunity of entering the hitherto protected Spanish domestic market in which INH was the only significant player. The company had to defend its position in Spain. INH had to be revitalised and eventually privatised.

Because of its size, as Spain's largest company, its high profile presence in every town and on every main highway in the country and because of its competitive position as Spain's chief player in the global oil world, Repsol had the opportunity to become the admired model for a revitalised dynamic and democratic Spain. Repsol could become and be seen as the new Spain's industrial and commercial flagship. This was the vision that was presented to and agreed by the board. This vision was made overt and explicit and became the brief upon which the new identity was based.

The naming structure and visual identity followed from this brief. The name INH was abandoned in favour of one of the brands, Repsol, and a monolithic identity structure was adopted in order to give the organisation strength and coherence. So traditional names in chemicals, exploration and distribution were abandoned. This was a move which caused considerable but temporary pain. The new visual idea had to be Spanish in feeling and appearance, but it also had to present the strength and sophistication of a major global oil company. This new identity was launched as part of a massive and on-going

internal and external communication programme –
in which a series of powerful, clear and simple messages have been reiterated. The identity programme
ran in parallel with a long-term behavioural change
programme.

Stage Two

Developing
the identity

As a result of the work carried out in the first stage, culminating in the presentation and the agreement of the vision/central idea, actions may be taken on the three interrelated areas:

- behavioural change
- structure
- name and visual style.

Behavioural change

There may be a requirement to develop a behavioural change programme based around the need to promulgate the new central idea/vision internally.

The process of introducing and managing behavioural change can be complex, difficult and prolonged. Depending on the size of the organisation and the level of the change required such a process can take up to three years.

A wide variety of organisational behaviour disciplines is available to corporations. Information about these can be obtained from publications, specialised consultancies and the Institute of Personnel Development

Identity structure

Issues to examine here are:

- Do we have or should we develop an endorsed, branded or monolithic identity structure?
- How do we make it work?

Sometimes, as in the case of Repsol, these issues almost resolve themselves; more often though the issues are complex and multi-faceted. Each possible solution has to be explored, and its advantages and drawbacks weighed up. For more detail refer to Section Three.

Name and visual style

Linked to structure is name and visual style. Should there be some change in what the organisation is called, how it looks and presents itself, either a minor change involving modification to the existing identity or something entirely new?

Name

Sometimes changing situations make name changes inevitable. It is instructive to look at examples from the nation-state. The Dutch East Indies became Indonesia in the late 1940s after 300 years of Dutch colonial rule and a bitter and bloody struggle. Rhodesia became Zimbabwe and its capital Salisbury became Harare for similar reasons a generation or so later. These countries changed their name to reinforce their changed status and position in the world.

Companies, like countries, change names when circumstances make it difficult or impossible for them to sustain their existing name. For example when Kuwait Petroleum International took over the retail Gulf oil network in Europe one of the conditions of the deal was that the name should change. That led to Wolff Olins creating Q8. When the French hotel and catering business Novotel merged with Jacques Borel neither party would accept the other's name so a new name was needed. Wolff Olins invented Accor.

Like symbols, names are emotive. Creating and introducing a new name is difficult and complex for the following reasons:

First, names have no real life or meaning until they are put into a context, so it is extremely difficult for the people going through the process to appreciate the power of the name until after the event.

Second, individual preferences and feelings are very important.

Third, a very large number of names are already registered and it is difficult to find 'free' names.

Fourth, names are a legal minefield. Name registration is complex and rights to the ownership of names are sometimes difficult to determine. Many names are owned, part-owned or can be claimed by organisations whose legal position is debatable. The legal processes involved in name change are vexatious and contentious.

Having said all that, there are, as always, a few guidelines in the development of names which might be helpful.

Types of name

Names can be classified under the following types.

First is the name of an individual or individuals, usually the company's founder, like Ford, Philips, Lucas, Marks & Spencer.

Second come descriptive names like British Airways or General Motors. Remember, though, that these sometimes become embarrassingly outdated. There was once a grocery chain called Home & Colonial Stores. Currently anything with the prefix Euro is fashionable.

Third are abbreviated names like Conoco and Preussag.

Fourth are initials for example KLM, IBM, ICI and BP.

first direct

Q8 and First Direct are two of the more memorable, appropriate and successful names created by Wolff Olins.

In the fifth category are names like Kodak or Viyella which are simply intended to look and sound unique and attractive.

Finally, in the sixth category are conceptual names, that is names that try to give an impression of what the organisation seeks to do, or to be – eg Jaguar, Accor, Cordiant.

Criteria

Here are the criteria for selecting a name. It should:

- be easy to read
- be easy to pronounce, preferably in any language
- have no disagreeable associations, preferably in any language
- be suitable for use as the organisation expands into different activities
- be registrable, or at least protectable
- not date
- if possible, relate to the activity of the company
- be idiosyncratic
- be something with which a powerful visual style can be associated
- have charisma.

Very few names will fit all these criteria. Although some of Wolff Olins' most successful programmes, for instance Accor, 3i, Q8, Kingfisher, Forte, Repsol, have been based around name change or modification, it remains the case that identity programmes involving name changes are

Solo is the electronic banking brand of the Merita, Finland's largest financial service group. The symbol, part of an identity programme by Wolff Olins, visualises the product concept in a clear and direct way.

Irish Life

The symbol of Irish Life, Ireland's largest insurance company is made up from a complex and allusive series of references to aspiration.

difficult. My advice on changing names is simple. Don't unless you really must.

Visual style

Some thoughts on symbols are outlined in Section One. Symbols, as much as, perhaps even more than names, arouse deep and sometimes conflicting emotions.

Organisations which have spent millions on promoting their symbols over years are more likely to wish to modify what they have than change completely – and they may well be right. Within the last two decades Renault, one of Europe's automotive giants, has modified its symbol and all its other visual manifestations twice, but the basic lozenge

shape of the symbol has remained. Shell, BP and ICI are three other companies that modulate rather than change. These modifications are simply intended to help keep the organisation up to date. In this sense then they can be regarded as exercises in corporate branding.

There are situations, however, when it is desirable to produce a new visual solution. This is especially necessary when an organisation is introducing a new corporate vision like, say, BT or Akzo. But here timing is a critical issue: the new identity must represent a new reality.

Always remember that a change of design makes a promise of changed performance which has to be fulfilled. The visual style must never promise more

than the organisation will be able to deliver. If it isn't delivered the organisation is deemed to be lying. The public and its spokespersons in the media are unforgiving on this issue and rightly so.

Design approaches

Once there is agreement on the extent of change required, the consultancy will prepare a series of optional design approaches which it will show in sketch form across an appropriate range of activities.

The chosen design scheme is then worked up for a presentation showing how the various applications will work on the exterior and interiors of buildings, advertising, literature, vehicles, uniforms and so on; multi-media applications are becoming increasingly important in this context.

The approved sketches must be developed into artwork and then fine tuned so that they are usable across a wide range of materials (eg plastics, paper, metal) and a wide range of sizes (eg buttonhole badges to neon signs) in a wide range of countries with differing technical facilities, by people inside and outside the company with varying skills, knowledge and interest.

First, basic elements are produced from artwork. (See Appendix A.)

Second, from these basic elements a wide range

of typical applications for use is prepared, covering, say, stationery, signs and shop interiors and multi-media. (See Appendix B.)

Manuals

The final design work is encapsulated in a manual which is intended to be the single source from which the tone and style of the organisation's work is set. Traditionally the manual is a document, sometimes quite slim, but often running to four or more volumes, showing how to use the identity. The manual sets out how everything that the organisation produces, from writing paper to signs on buildings to vehicle liveries, should be made and how it should look.

The manual usually also enshrines an 'onwards and upwards' message from the Chairman or Chief Executive. In this case the manual, or as it is sometimes so meaningfully called, 'The Bible', inevitably tries to balance on the tightrope between the practical and the spiritual, but since it cannot effectively operate both as an instruction document and Holy Writ, it often falls somewhere between the two.

Although there have been experiments in all kinds of printed manuals from formal and rigid to informal, chatty and flexible, most fail, in the sense that the people who most need them – printers, sign makers and other craft-based operators – find them clumsy, inflexible and often irrelevant.

Electronic manuals

Now, through information technology, manuals can be created electronically and flow through the corporate information technology system. They can become infinitely flexible and ubiquitous. They can be adapted and updated with ease. They can be on-line. In other words they can be on everyone's desk.

And this means that the identity programme can emerge everywhere and adapt easily to every conceivable situation.

Electronic manuals represent a huge step in the use of identity as a mainstream and, above all, easy to use management resource.

Brand book
Livre de la marque
Libro de la marca

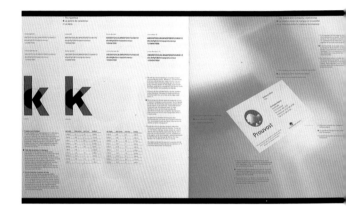

Printed identity manuals come in all shapes, sizes and levels of sophistication. Shown here is a simple, attractive practical manual for the Prouvost Division of the French multinational Chargeurs, for whom Wolff Olins created an identity programme. Prouvost has operations in wool throughout the world. The clouds symbol is of course a visual pun on wool.

Launch and introduction – communicating the vision

Communication is the key to creating and sustaining understanding of the new vision and its accompanying identity.

The launch of a new identity gives management an opportunity to explain what the organisation is, where it has come from, where it is going and how the new identity will help it get there. The visual identity becomes the vehicle that launches the vision or the new corporate brand, or whatever else has been planned.

For many organisations the launch of the new identity can represent a rite of passage, a kind of rebirth, and it may therefore be appropriate to make it into an elaborate and ritualised occasion.

On the other hand some organisations may feel that this quasi-religious approach is inappropriate to their ethos. Each organisation must choose what is natural to it.

Internal launch

The internal launch of an identity programme takes place before the external launch, because people inside the organisation have to know about it first if they are to feel that it is really theirs. If it is linked to a major organisational change, say a merger, involving a new name and identity, for months before the launch change groups should have worked together in order to inculcate and explain the new central idea, spirit or vision of the new organisation. The internal launch of the new visual identity should be the climax of this process.

The internal launch normally takes the form of seminars, discussions and audiovisual presentations. It can be a complex and sophisticated presentation with all the high-tech skills of a world-class stage or TV show, complete with well known personalities, or a much lower key activity. This depends on the message, the corporate ethos and tradition, and similar matters.

Many of the world's great organisations now devote much time and energy to communication. Ford, for instance, has its own internal TV networks for dissemination of corporate policy, news of new model launches and so on. Where significant communication channels exist they have to be used as vehicles to launch the identity and propagate the vision/central idea; where they don't exist these communication channels have to be created.

Dealer/distributor launch

Although the dealer/distributor is not part of the corporate entity, his success (as in cars or soft drink bottling) is often bound up with the fortunes of the organisation with which he deals. Launches to dealers are therefore much more akin to internal launches than those for external audiences.

External launch

Nobody should expect the outside world to be as interested in the new identity as insiders – unless it is deliberately aimed at creating a new corporate brand for customers.

The external launch involves advertising, brochures, multi-media techniques, sales meetings and often a quite complex press relations programme. It is sometimes suitable to use sophisticated audiovisual techniques at such events.

The appropriate consultants in advertising, public relations, multi-media events and so on must be co-opted into the programme to handle these activities.

Stage Four

Implementation – making it happen

The new logo (by Wolff Olins) which replaced the old-fashioned triangle.

Making change stick

When it is carried out thoroughly, the identity process is deeply satisfying because it does make change happen. If the programme is introduced and implemented wholeheartedly and enthusiastically it will completely change the way in which the organisation sees itself and is seen by others. It will help the organisation to do things that it could never have done before.

In an interview in *The European* newspaper on 28 April 1994, Arnout Loudon, who was retiring after 12 years as the president of Akzo, 'remembered the introduction of the logo which replaced an old fashioned triangle as his most personal victory at Akzo: "it was a difficult battle within the management council. In the end, this daring decision turned out to be a success, but it could just as easily have gone the other way". During the 1980's Loudon and his team laid out a strategy to drastically rearrange the portfolio of the company by getting rid of loss-making or non-core activities and strengthening the company's business in more attractive sectors like speciality chemicals, coatings and the pharmaceuticals industry.' All this was predicated around the introduction of the new identity.

'As soon as the corporate identity had been established, the management divided the products into 3 categories: half were seen as strong, 40% were potentially strong and 10% were undeniably weak.' The new identity was the basis from which the new organisation began to emerge.

Another striking example which demonstrates how identity change releases energy and helps to drive up efficiency and profitability is BT – now one of the world's leading telecoms businesses. The launch of the identity was timed to coincide with the emergence of a newer, leaner, more sophisticated, efficient and profitable organisation. The new identity of BT not only proclaimed change, but was a catalyst in making change happen.

Just to take a couple of other examples with which Wolff Olins has been involved in the financial field: 3i and the Prudential became and were seen to become completely different organisations after their identity programmes began to emerge, from what they had both been before. The new identity released an energy which enabled these organisations not just to look different but to perform and operate in a much more effective and powerful fashion.

Identity work, perhaps more than any other kind of consultancy, does make change happen.

Managing implementation

Like any other corporate resource the successful management of identity depends on the effort and enthusiasm with which it is introduced and managed. Because identity is a corporate resource embracing products and services, environments, communication and behaviour, each of which must be incorporated into the identity management process (see Section One of this Guide), it has to be managed on lines similar to those two other corporate resources, finance and information

systems (see Section Five of this Guide). It has to be ubiquitous; it must penetrate every part of the organisation. And in order to do this effectively, it has to have both a formal and an informal structure, and both formal and informal support systems.

Formal identity management systems

The formal implementation management programme will normally be based around a Head of Identity who may also be Head of Design, Head of Communication or occasionally even Head of Human Resources. Whatever he/she is called, this person will have representatives reporting in from most of the operating units and central functions. He/she will liaise on a regular basis with marketing, design and human resource people.

The identity team will see to it that appropriate standards are maintained in stationery, signs, packaging and all other visual areas, including architecture. The team will work with suppliers of all kinds to create and sustain appropriate standards. The design manual, whether electronic with its instant on-line access or in its less accessible printed form, will be a fundamental tool of this team.

In addition the identity will have an impact on all new activities of whatever kind, from commissioning a new building to acquiring a new subsidiary. As the organisation changes, moves into new activities and develops new products, the identity must be used appropriately and modified where necessary. For example, if a financial services organisation uses new technology to develop a new customer service, the brand people involved must work with the identity resource to produce an effective and appropriate corporate brand. First Direct is an example of this.

From time to time there will be a conflict of interest or opinion. As in any dispute between a corporate resource and a division this should be resolved by arbitration.

Informal management

So much for the formal part of the programme. At a fundamental and in some ways more significant level, however, the identity programme is to do with emotion; creating and sustaining a feeling about what is appropriate for the organisation, demonstrating a consistency of purpose (see Section One). In the most successful identity programmes everything that the organisation does or says represents what it is and underlines its identity. And this is not just because there is a formal policing structure, but because there is an all-pervasive spirit which every-

one within the organisation intuitively understands. Any close examination of organisations which use their identity properly will confirm this. Companies with a powerful and well implemented identity know that the identity resource helps them achieve their objectives; therefore they respect it, some may even treasure it. All this of course stems from the top. When the Chairman or Chief Executive guards the identity and cherishes it, the rest of the organisation follows. Marks & Spencer is often and quite properly cited as an organisation which guards all aspects of its identity with this kind of care.

In addition to this, the identity which should so clearly outline the shape and structure of the organisation and give visual expression to its strategy constantly reminds management where its goals lie, and what is and is not appropriate for it to do. An effective identity programme is the corporate strategy made visible.

Forte hotels embrace every category from the exclusive Ritz in Madrid to your local Travelodge. The flexible identity system, offers the maximum diversity and choice within a coherent whole.

Flexibility

Does all this mean that the organisation has to become an unyielding, inflexible, invasive giant? Not necessarily.

A good deal of criticism has been levelled at identity programmes for introducing a kind of bland homogeneity across everything that they touch. High streets are said to be increasingly similar; so are the world's airports and so on. It has to be said that much of this criticism is justified. In the world of oil companies, for example, simply to make every service station everywhere in the world look the same in the interest of immediate recognition and economies of scale is to ignore, even to obliterate, the joy that we all take in variety and difference and the goodwill that consumers develop towards the organisation that offers them diversity. By the same token it is neither necessary nor desirable for every bank branch regardless of whether it is in a small country town, a shopping mall or a major financial centre to look exactly the same. There is a compelling case for variety within consistency.

Some organisations are beginning to recognise that diversity of offerings within a coherent and consistent framework makes an attractive commercial offer. In the Forte Hotels identity system five different combinations of hotel type are offered within a coherent, corporate context.

It is also clear that the identity will need to be modulated and adapted from time to time according to the changing circumstances which the organisation faces. Information technology is making this opportunity for greater variety quite readily available at a cost which is not exorbitant. Like every other management tool, identity has to be used with discretion, care and an appropriate lightness of touch.

Control, cost and timing

Methods of control and costing

An economical resource

Identity is an economical management resource, because it operates mainly through the activities which an organisation conducts on a regular basis; for the most part identity involves very little new or additional expenditure. Buildings have to be painted, signs have to be put up, vehicles have to be acquired and put into an appropriate livery, brands have to be launched, training has to take place, and so on. All this is co-ordinated by the identity programme.

Of course there are some additional costs – consultants' fees, launch costs, advertising the new programme – but they are relatively small in relation to the impact of the whole.

Budgeting

Corporate identity costs are, apart from the origination work, usually dealt with as part of annual departmental budgets. So far as the visual part of the identity is concerned signs get repainted, stationery gets reprinted, vehicles get replaced.

Then there are all the costs involved in behavioural change. Some of these, such as training and the use of existing communication channels, involve little or no extra cost but some may be new.

Costs can be divided up and examined in the following way:

- consultants' fees
- cost of creating new materials
  (eg signs on buildings)

The retail identity for Vauxhall dealers, part of the identity programme by Wolff Olins, has created higher customer interest and greater sales volume than its predecessors.

- cost of launching the identity (eg advertising, videos etc)
- replacement costs – those costs involved in replacing existing materials which would have needed replacing anyway (eg stationery, vehicle liveries etc)
- costs for communication and training.

Each programme should be costed in stages. A fixed budget for time and fees should be established for Stages One and Two. Variations should be allowed for if the brief changes. There should be a clear separation between fees and outside costs.

Fees for Stages Three and Four should be negotiated as the project develops and its total approximate size can be estimated.

During the course of Stage Three, and more particularly during implementation (Stage Four), fees can be negotiated for separate projects.

Special programmes like a new corporate brand are of course treated as one-off projects.

Controls

The corporate identity resource has to be established with a clear brief, adequate funding and appropriate lines of authority. Here are some of the issues that have to be resolved:

- Who is going to pay for the programme – the centre or the operating units?
- How should liaison between different companies or sectors, geographic divisions and the central identity resource work?
- How should the resource be manned and how many staff should it have?
- Where should it be located?
- What are the lines of responsibility?

A cost, time and method schedule for the launch and subsequent management of the programme must be prepared at the same time as detailed preparation work is taking place. This will be monitored regularly and it will almost certainly be modified from time to time.

Size, scope, speed and cost

At what speed is the implementation programme going to be introduced and sustained? There are four choices:

- an overnight change from old to new
- a controlled change taking place very quickly, say over a period of a year
- a controlled but more gradual change, say over 3–5 years
- gradual replacement on an ad hoc basis.

Quite reasonably most organisations like to keep costs down so where possible they will choose the longer, slower, cheaper option. However, the method chosen must depend on the nature of the identity change: the more dramatic the change, the more rapidly the new identity should be introduced, and inevitably the higher the cost will be.

If a large-scale programme involves a new vision, a new name, a new visual identity and so on, there will be requirement for massive impact at high speed. When Gulf Oil changed to Q8 we simply could not leave the petrol stations in two different liveries with two different sets of names over a long period of time. The change had to take place fast. Three and a half thousand outlets were changed in six countries over a three-month period.

The identity programme for Vauxhall involves product, environment, communication and behaviour. It is regarded by the company as a long-term investment. The picture shows the front grille of Vauxhall cars (1995).

When, as is often the case, the existing identity is modified, the introduction can be lower key, the programme of implementation more gradual, and therefore the costs can be lower and spread out over a longer period.

Example

The identity programme for Vauxhall Motors may be more typical. The new Vauxhall identity programme was launched to capitalise on major improvements in the product. The image of Vauxhall as a company had to improve in line with the quality of the car.

Identity for Vauxhall is not an additional overhead; it is part of corporate investment which, like product investment, is on-going.

Identity is simply a part of the organisation's continuous improvement programme. Implementation costs are normally treated as part of standard annual expenditure budgets.

One important exception was the programme to re-design, improve and upgrade dealerships – now known as retailers. The programme took about four years; costs were split between manufacturer and retailer. The changes were radical; 550 dealers were involved.

As the Vauxhall example shows it is more useful to treat identity as long-term investment rather than an annual expense.

Section Nine

Research

There are two separate issues to consider here. The first is to research whether the proposed identity programme is acceptable to the various audiences at whom it is aimed. This means pre-testing names and designs. And the second is to find out whether the identity programme is succeeding in raising favourable awareness of the organisation.

Researching name and visual style

Is it practical to research the proposed identity programme before it is launched?

There are differing views on this. One respectable view is that it is possible to research individual parts of the proposed identity programme – names, colours, symbols and even the whole – before it is launched. The argument goes that such research, while it may not tell you what will work, will definitely tell you what won't. Client organisations increasingly demand that research of this kind should be undertaken. As research techniques improve, it is clear that the risk-reduction process which this kind of activity offers is becoming increasingly worthwhile.

Some research is vital. It is essential to go through all the proper procedures to check that any new names which may be proposed are both available and culturally and linguistically acceptable wherever the organisation operates. It is also important to understand that certain colours and shapes have specific implications in different parts of the world. Many organisations feel that informal discussions with a representative sample of internal and external client contacts world-wide is a helpful

and economical way of dealing with this issue.

Where packaging is changed, shops are redesigned or some other direct and clear marketing change is made, the normal commercial risk-reduction procedures involving research must be undertaken.

Researching impact – tracking studies

Most organisations quite reasonably want to know whether their new identity programme has worked. Their questions are: What did I get for what I spent? What did people think of my organisation before? What do they think of it now?

So after a programme has been launched, some companies carry out tracking studies to check the extent to which the new identity programme has affected the attitude of different groups of people towards the organisation. Research of this kind is well tried and for the most part pretty reliable. It will not only tell you what target audiences think of the identity, but much more importantly what they think of the organisation and how their perceptions have changed over time.

Risks

All change involves risk. Identity change inevitably involves some element of risk too. However, the decision to change or modify identity normally arises because changes in the organisation's environment have provoked the organisation to reconsider its positioning. The identity change is one of the manifestations of change which the organisation has to undertake in order to survive successfully. This is the light in which risks should be regarded.

I have outlined two major risks to the successful implementation of an identity programme at various points in this Guide.

In summary these are:

First, that the organisation creates and launches an identity programme which promises more than it can deliver. Nothing creates more scepticism than an organisation which claims to have changed when it hasn't. (See Section Seven.)

Second, that the organisation launches the programme but does not sustain it. Different parts of the organisation ignore the new identity, modify it to suit themselves – or even implicitly ridicule it, thereby bringing it into contempt. In this case it is usually perceived by those who come into contact with it as a superficial and cosmetic exercise.

In other words there is much more risk in handling an identity badly internally than from any external threat.

Acknowledgments

The New Wolff Olins Guide to Identity is based around the experience related to the 200 or so major identity programmes that Wolff Olins has carried out since it was started as one of the pioneering identity consultancies in 1965.

The thoughts and methodologies outlined in it derive largely from our current operational practice.

I would like to thank all my colleagues in Wolff Olins both past and present for all their work both in developing the identity discipline and in helping to articulate it. I would like to thank five of my present colleagues particularly: Brian Boylan for his reflections on the relationship between internal and external manifestations of identity and identity as a change management tool, John Banks for help in organisational behaviour, John Williamson for his thoughts on vision, Keshen Teo for designing the Guide and Tarnia De Val for endlessly typing and retyping it as it changed and developed.

Finally I hope you will find this edition of the Guide useful in your work.

Illustration credits

Bibliography

Here are a few books which a reader on the subject may find both interesting and useful. The books chosen deal not only with design, but also with business, history and art. All these are proper subjects for the study of identity.

Aaker, D.A.
Managing Brand Equity: Capitalizing on the Value of a Brand Name
The Free Press, 1991

Aldersey-Williams, H.
Corporate Identity
Lund Humphries, London, 1994

Buddensieg, T.
Industriekultur, Peter Behrens and the AEG
MIT Press, 1984 (Eng translation)

Banham, R.
Theory and Design in the First Machine Age
Architectural Press, 1960

Barrett, G. (ed)
Forensic Marketing
McGraw-Hill, 1995

Bartlett, C.A. and Ghoshal, S.
Managing Across Borders
Harvard Business School Press, 1989

Baumeister, F.
Identity, Cultural Change and the Struggle for Self
Oxford University Press, 1986

Bernstein, D.
Company Image and Reality
Architectural Press,
Holt, Rinehart & Winston, 1984

Betjeman, J.
London's Historic Railway Stations
John Murray, 1972

Birkigt, K. and Stadler, M.M.
Corporate Identity, Grundlagen, Funktionen und Beispielen
Verlag, Moderne Industrie, 1986

Bos,B. et al
The Image of a Company
Architecture Design and Technology Press, 1990

Bowers, M.
Railway Styles in Building
Almark, 1975

Campbell, J.
The Power of Myth
Doubleday, 1988

Campbell, J.
The Hero with a Thousand Faces
Sphere, 1975

Caplan, R.
By Design
St Martin's Press, 1982

Colley, L.
Britons: Forging the Nation 1707-1837
Pimlico 1994

Cox, A.
Straight Talk for Monday Morning, Creating Values, Vision and Vitality at Work
Wiley, 1990

Handy, C.
Understanding Organisations
Penguin, 1986

Handy, C.
The Empty Raincoat
Hutchinson, 1994

Heller, R.
The New Naked Manager
Hodder & Stoughton, rev ed, 1985
(most of Heller's books are worth reading)

Hobsbawm, E. and Ranger, T.
The Invention of Tradition
Cambridge University Press, 1983

Howard, M.
The Lessons of History
Oxford University Press, 1993

Hudson, L.
Contrary Imaginations
Penguin, 1968

Koestler, P.
The Act of Creation
Hutchinson, 1976

Kotler, P.
Marketing Management: Analysis, Planning, Implementation and Control
Prentice Hall, 1994

Kuhn, T.S.
The Structure of the Scientific Revolution
University of Chicago, 1970

Levitt, T.
The Marketing Imagination
The Free Press, 1983

Lorenz, C.
Design Dimensions
Basil Blackwell, 1986

Murphy, J.M.
Branding – A Key Marketing Tool
Macmillan, 1987

Napoles, V.
Corporate Identity Design
Van Nostrand Reinhold, 1988

Ohmae, K.
The Borderless World
Collins, 1990

Olins, W.
Corporate Identity
Thames & Hudson, 1989

Olins, W. (ed)
International Corporate Identity
Laurence King Publishing, 1995

Papanek, V.
Design for the Real World
Thames & Hudson, 2nd ed, 1985

Pevsner, N.
Pioneers of Modern Design
Penguin, 2nd ed, 1960

Pffaf, W
The Wrath of Nations
Touchstone - Simon and Schuster, 1994

Pilditch, J.
I'll be over in the morning
Mercury Business Books, 1990

Pilditch, J.
Talk about Design
Barrie & Jenkins, 1976

Porter, M.
Competitive Advantage
Collier Macmillan, 1985

Prendergast, M.
For God, Country and Coca-Cola
Phoenix, 1994

Quinn, M.
The Swastika, Constructing the Symbol
Routledge, 1994

Rolt, L.T.C.
Isambard Kingdom Brunel
Penguin, 1985

Schultz, M.
On Studying Organisational Cultures
Walter de Gryter, 1995

Schultz, D.E. Tannenbaum, S.I.
and Lauterborn, A.F.
*Integrated Marketing Communication:
Pulling it all together and making it work*
N.T.C. Business Books, 1993

Selame, E. and Selame, J.
The Company Image
Wiley, 1988

Simon, A.
The Science of the Artificial
MIT Press, 1981

Sloan, A.
My years with General Motors
Doubleday & Co, New York, 1984

Steckel, R.
*Filthy Rich and other non-profit fantasies – Changing
the way non-profits do business in the 90's*
Ten Speed Press, 1988

Storr, A.
The Dynamics of Creation
Penguin, 1976

Trevor-Roper, H.
*Princes and Artists: Patronage and Ideology of Four
Habsburg Courts 1577–1633*
Thames & Hudson, 1976

Van Riel, C.B.M.
Principles of Corporate Communication
Prentice Hall, 1995

Whitfield, R.R.
Creativity in Industry
Penguin, 1975

Wiener, M.
*English Culture and the Decline of the
Industrial Spirit 1850–1980*
Cambridge University Press, 1982

Appendix A – The Basic Elements

These are the basic elements that make up the visual system of a corporate identity:

- name
- subsidiary names (if appropriate)
- symbol
- main typeface
- subsidiary typefaces (if appropriate)
- colours

Appendix B – Checklist for Visual Audit

This is a standard checklist of items over which the visual elements are usually applied. Experience indicates that it is appropriate for most companies, but it may need modifying in particular cases.

Products and Services

Products
- product design
- product identification
- rating plates
- operating instructions
- calibration instructions

Packaging
- inners
- outer cartons
- labelling
- delivery instructions
- installation instructions

Environments

Interiors/Exteriors
- buildings
- reception areas
- sales areas
- offices
- factories
- shops
- showrooms

Signs
- main identification
- general sign system, internal/external

Exhibitions

Clothing
- badges
- safety hats
- overalls
- lab coats
- smocks

Communication materials

Stationery
- letterheads
- continuation sheets
- memos
- compliment slips
- visiting cards
- envelopes
- postal labels

Forms
- accounting
- purchasing
- sales
- production
- personnel

Publications
- corporate
- personnel/training
- industry packages
- product

Vehicles
- road transport
- factory transport

Advertising
- corporate
- recruitment
- product/services

Promotions/Giveaways
- flags
- stickers
- ties
- promotional and point-of-sale material

Appendix C - Audiences

Internal and quasi-internal audiences

- All staff, at all levels, in all companies and divisions, in all countries
- Families of employees
- Representatives of trade unions
- Shareholders
- Directors
- Pensioners

External audiences

These are some of the main external audiences:

- Central government, local government, regional government
- Competitors
- Suppliers
- Customers, both direct and indirect
- Opinion formers
- Journalists
- Investment analysts, merchant bankers, stockbrokers
- Potential recruits
- Schools and universities
- Trade and industry associations

Appendix D – Design Advisory Services

The Chartered Society of Designers (CSD)
29 Bedford Square
London WC1B 3EG
0171 631 1510

Design Business Association
29 Bedford Square
London WC1B 3EG
0171 631 1510

The Design Council
Haymarket House
1 Oxendon Street
London SW1Y 4EE
0171 839 8000

Design Management Institute
364 Brookline Avenue
Boston Mass 02215
(617) 236 4165

Incorporated Society of British Advertisers (ISBA)
44 Hertford Street
London W1Y 8AE
0171 499 7502

Institute of Public Relations (IPR)
The Old Trading House
15 Northburgh Street
London EC1V 0PR
0171 253 5151

Appendix E – How Identity Helps

Any identity programme will not succeed by itself in making change. An effective identity underlines change, helps it to happen and continually reminds the organisation what its goals are.

The benefits which a corporate identity programme can bring must therefore always be seen as part of a package of corporate changes and improvements.

With this proviso the benefits which a change in corporate identity can bring are as follows:

- It allows the process of change to take place more quickly and easily inside an organisation
- It enables one company to absorb another with the minimum dislocation
- It enables organisations to tell the people with whom they deal what they stand for, what they are, what they do and how they do it. It enables them to explain how their activities relate to each other
- It encourages tighter and more coherent messages of all kinds to emerge from the corporation
- It enables people who deal with the company to understand its corporate goals and objectives

Because of these advantages, a well organised corporate identity programme also brings with it other advantages

Internal

- It can improve morale and motivation
- It can reduce staff turnover
- It can enable better products of more consistent quality to be produced
- It can enable the company to attract a better calibre of employee than its more anonymous competitors
- It can enable people from different parts of the organisation to work together more effectively

Financial

- It can make for higher recognition in financial circles, and therefore often favourably affects share prices
- It can allow acquisitions to be made with less difficulty
- It can allow organisations to defend them selves more effectively against potential predators

Marketing

- It can encourage consumers to look more favourably upon the company and its products and to stay brand-loyal
- It can encourage suppliers to operate regularly and consistently
- It can allow for more cost-effective expenditure in terms of activities and promotion
- It can enable the company to establish itself more effectively in new markets
- It can allow for the more rapid emergence of new activities within a company

Index

Learning Resources
Centre